MW01136733

WHAT WILL PEOPLE THINK?

HOW TO BE CONFIDENT IN YOURSELF AND STOP WORRYING ABOUT WHAT PEOPLE THINK

ROMA SHARMA

FIRST EDITION, SELF-PUBLISHED BY ROMA SHARMA
PRINTED IN INDIA

ISBN 978-93-5419-596-9

DISCLAIMER

While all attempts have been made to verify the information provided in this publication, neither author nor the publisher assumes any responsibility for errors, omissions or interpretations on the subject matter herein.

This book is for informational purposes only. The views expressed are those of the author alone and should be implemented by the reader at his/her own responsibility. The information provided is of a general nature only. Inferences from examples, suggestions and opinions are made based on the experiences of the author and should not be used as a substitute for professional opinion. The views expressed in this book should not be taken as expert instructions or commands.

The reader is entirely responsible for his/her own actions. Stories, examples and anecdotes provided in this book are fictional and any resemblance to any person is purely coincidental.

The author does not tend to imply any particular problem or situation to be related specifically to the male gender or the female one. The gender neutrality of the characters needs to be maintained on part of the reader and the context needs to be seen irrespective of the gender being used.

Adherence to all applicable laws and regulations including international, federal, state and local governing professional licensing, business practices, advertising and all other aspects of doing business in any jurisdiction is the sole responsibility of the reader or purchaser. Neither the author nor the publisher assumes any responsibility or liability whatsoever on the behalf of the purchaser or reader of these materials.

CONTENTS

DOWNLOAD YOUR FREE 'BEING YOURSELF JOURNAL'

Your
FREE Book!

BEING
YOURSELF
JOURNAL

ROMA SHARMA

For more books log onto
romasharma.com

Subscribe to my newsletter and receive a FREE copy of the **Being Yourself Journal** with powerful self-coaching questions. Log onto **romasharma.com**

Here is what you will find in the journal:

1. Page templates that you can fill out every day to connect with your thoughts and feelings
2. Affirmations to increase self-esteem and confidence
3. Self-coaching questions that will help you find solutions in difficult situations
4. Simple ways to decrease worry and stay calm in the present moment

As you continue to read the book, **What will people think?** you will find self-coaching questions present in different sections. Download the complete set of questions provided in the **Being Yourself Journal** and refer to it while reading this book for best results.

Download now! Log onto **romasharma.com**

Do you also want to discover the habits of thinking that can lead to your definite success?

In the book, **Thinking Habits For Definite Success**, you will find a step-by-step guide to develop a success mindset that can transform your career, health, and relationships.

Also By Roma

Log onto romasharma.com to discover the full series.

What readers say about **Thinking Habits For Definite Success**:

"Inspirational examples explained logically"

"Recommended to anyone looking for a life-changing experience"

Log onto romasharma.com and buy your copy of **Thinking Habits For Definite Success** today!

ONLINE COURSES

The Complete Guide to Finding Your Perfect Partner

Would you like to have lifetime access to my video training courses at 80% OFF? Please find the discount coupons here:

romasharma.com/courses

1

WHAT WILL PEOPLE THINK? AN INTRODUCTION

Have you noticed people who are relaxed, calm and confident in their skin and wondered if they are doing something different inside their mind? What makes some people satisfied with the way they are while others strive hard to create an alternate image of themselves— one they hope will be liked by others?

As a coach and trainer in the field of emotional well-being, I have been conducting individual coaching sessions and group training programs since 2014. I have had the opportunity of spending hours listening to the deepest thoughts and feelings of people—their dreams, aspirations, beliefs and issues.

A few years ago, I decided to compile the thought process and underlying beliefs of my clients who were able to get the results they wanted for themselves. I also found a common factor among clients who found it difficult to move towards their goals with complete conviction—they seemed to care more for what other people thought of them rather than what they wanted for themselves. Be it their dreams of stepping into a unique profession, finding a partner they liked or just doing something they are passionate about, their concern for how they would be perceived by others seemed to outweigh their desire to manifest their goals.

My objective behind writing this book is to give a complete blueprint of what works best if people want to achieve their goals but are restricted by the judgment and opinions of others.

Although each one of us is unique, at some level, we are all the same. We all want to feel loved and accepted. We all have a little child inside us that is scared of rejection. Sometimes the fear of being rejected prevents us from living our greater life—one that allows us to embrace our true self and gives us the joy of being the unique individuals that we really are.

In this book, you will discover:

- The 7 best ways to stop caring about what other people think
- How to follow your dreams with confidence and certainty despite the judgment of others
- How to deal with conflicting opinions without compromising your relationships
- The strategies we use to read people's minds and how to overcome the unwanted effects
- Why trying to please people actually makes them like you less
- The primary fear that makes us concerned about people's views about us and the best ways to deal with it
- Time-tested ways to create a great image of yourself on auto-pilot while being yourself, authentically and unapologetically.
- The counter-intuitive reason behind why people try to control or manipulate you

I have had the privilege of journeying with my clients and watching them become very successful in their goals by working on themselves. These experiences have helped me understand people and the state of mind that has led to their success. I have not disclosed any details of my clients in this book as I am bound by confidentiality. However, I have used hypothetical situations and done my best to pass on my observation of what has worked well for them.

By the end of this book, you will be free from the question: *what will people think?* I am very excited to share my observations with you. So without further delay, let's dive in.

WHY IS WHAT PEOPLE THINK IMPORTANT?

We live in an ecosystem which entails give and take in our relationships. That's the only way for us to survive. It's important to us that other people like us. Life just becomes easier that way. We don't have to live in the uncertainty of *'Do they like me?'* or *'Don't they like me?'*. We just know and we can get on with our lives. When we do things that other people don't approve of, the contention saps us of our energy. Getting people to understand our perspective or to accept it can be quite exhausting. When we don't want to spend that kind of energy, we try to play it safe by just doing what they think is right.

The Reptilian Brain

Conforming to the group's expectation is a primal instinct. It comes from the two-million-year-old brain in us called the *reptilian brain*. If an animal was left out of the group, it could end up being eaten up by other animals or could fall prey to some other calamity. To ensure the survival of their species, animals developed what is known as the *herd mentality* according to which *staying together* was a way of *surviving together*. This is applicable even today. Our reptilian brain considers the opinions of people around us to be important. As a result, we might do things we never really wanted to do, in order to gain approval from others, in turn, sacrificing ourselves. That way, we sign up for short-term gain and long-term loss.

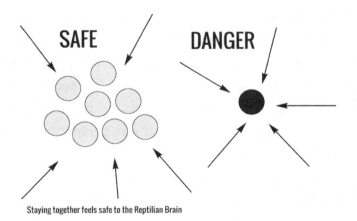

Staying together feels safe to the Reptilian Brain

We can see how advertising and marketing leverage on this point to sell to us. They show a person flaunting beautiful hair or driving an amazing car that makes heads turn in admiration. When onlookers are in awe of this person it makes us believe that their product will help us have a great public image too (one that they know is important to us!).

Approval Seeking as a Child

Sometimes the need to satisfy others could be really strong. This happens particularly if, during childhood, the parents were too strict, over-reacted when the baby made mistakes or had high expectations. A baby doesn't have a way to survive but to hope that her parents love and accept her, in the absence of which, she could feel really threatened. Her fear makes her feel like she is constantly walking on eggshells. She could become extremely adaptive and start doing things her parents want just so that she wouldn't displease them. This becomes a way of life, so she rarely thinks about what she needs. The focus is on pleasing the parents because that's the safest thing to do.

Rejection feels like death to an infant. When the baby grows into an adult, this child state continues to be in her. The approval of parents or primary caregivers is important, failing to receive which she could go through life seeking it in others and feeling the pain of rejection every time she doesn't get it.

The difficult parent is no longer around but is replaced by other people. These people have different faces but similar traits. She now tries to gain their approval in her life and continues to feel anxious when it comes to confronting them in any way. It makes her increasingly remorseful as her needs are not being met. She does not want to attract people who are like her difficult parents but that's what she unconsciously does because that is familiar to her and whatever is familiar feels safe.

It's important to note that the approval of *everyone* is not equally important to us. There is different weightage given to the approval of different people in our lives based on where we have placed them in our self-defined hierarchy.

Identity Decides Weightage

When it comes to people we look up to it is difficult for us to ignore their opinions. These could be people who care for us deeply or were there for us through thick and thin. We love them so much that we can not see them hurt in any way. Their opinions are as important to us as our own, maybe more.

When we care for a person's opinion it implies that he/she has a certain identity in our world. The more we regard this person the higher is the value placed on his/her perception. For instance, you might have been praised by a subordinate and it felt good. However, an appreciative comment from a person you look up to in your supervisor's circle might have meant more.

Identity decides the weightage given to an opinion. The greater the identity, the more the weightage.

This also implies that if you create an identity for yourself in somebody's world, your opinions will gain more credibility. You will be in a position to influence that person easily.

When there is conflict with people who mean a lot to us, we might end up doing things only to make them happy. In this case, we need to remember that the responsibility for what we are doing is ours, not theirs! The moment we shift the responsibility onto them we lose power and enter the dreaded game of hurt, pain, disappointment and shame.

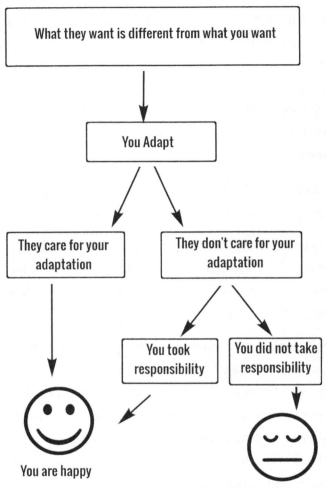

When we are caught in the middle of conflicting opinions, it helps to hash things out and find a middle ground. This can be done by asking others for what we need and at the same time being mindful of their needs. If the needs of any one side become more important than the other, it creates an imbalance in the relationship. If we are always adapting to what they want, we feel mistreated. If they are always adapting to what we want, they feel mistreated. A balance between the two sides brings stability to the relationship.

Being considerate about what people want is not the same as trying to please them. It's not possible for people to *become* happy with us without their mental participation in it. So, if we are more invested in the relationship than the other person is, it doesn't assure that the person will return our love and affection. In a relationship, we need both people to participate. One person can not decide to run the relationship. Hence, the expectations from our adjustments will need to be set as such. It helps to find a way that is mutually beneficial and take responsibility for what happens next.

Being Confident in Yourself

Adapting beyond a certain point to others creates a perception of you which could result in more expectations of adjustment coming your way. Hence, adapting needs to be done in moderation while continuously observing the results of doing so. When you don't worry about what people think, you reclaim your power and become attractive to those who desire this quality.

People like people who are like them or like someone they want to be. If I am anxious and I meet a relaxed person, it's natural for me to like that person. I might also wonder what makes him/her so easy going because I want that quality at some level. We don't pursue people as much as we pursue the energy they emit—something that they have and we want. People who like themselves and are not caught up in others perceptions of them can be great to be around. That's how we can create an amazing image of ourselves—by not trying too hard to do it! Counter-intuitive, isn't it?

When you don't try to control others and achieve what you want anyway, your confidence goes up through the roof. You feel it and others feel it too!

There are many merits to having a great public image. It helps us coexist with others in our ecosystems, gets us promotions and perks at our workplace and invitations to connect with more people socially. However, the problems begin when this image that is being created becomes very different from who we really are and unfortunately more important too. It's tiring as a lot of energy is spent in holding up that self-created image.

There are easier ways to create a good image on auto-pilot. For instance, we can demonstrate qualities of care and understanding towards others, which will help us create a good image without trying to do so. Care needs to be taken to ensure that we develop these qualities genuinely at a personality level and not superficially, intending to get something from others. If that is the case, people will sense it sooner or later. The relationship that could have been developed as a result of our good image will not stand a chance and the behavior to understand others will be viewed with skepticism.

So how can we confidently be ourselves, not worry about others and at the same time effortlessly create a great image? We are going to deal with every aspect of this in the upcoming sections. Let's start with understanding how we create our interpreted reality and what we can do to modify it in our favor.

3

MIND READING: A FORM OF HALLUCINATION

Mind reading is a distortion based on which we believe that we know what another person is thinking or feeling. Virginia Satir (1916-1988), an eminent family therapist, observed this in her practice. She said that when people communicate with others they tend to hallucinate about the other person's side of the story and pass it off as a fact. After one point, they can not tell the difference between what is *imagined* and what actually *is*—they both seem like one and the same.

a̋

Ted is hosting a party to which his best friend Eric has not been invited. Eric discovers this from their common friends and is disappointed. He believes that Ted doesn't like him and that is why he has not invited him. Ted on the other hand is feeling terrible about not inviting Eric. The party was being hosted for the college football team. He had requested Eric to join the team so that they could spend more time together. He was upset that Eric didn't care enough to apply. He believes that Eric doesn't like him either.

They both assumed that they knew what the other was thinking.

Mind reading or thinking on behalf of others can be quite tricky. People's thought process is a result of millions of bits of information that they are carrying around inside of them—not something specific that we can second guess. Their thinking engine is fueled by their own values, beliefs, decisions, memories and several other environmental factors that lead to certain ways of perceiving situations. It's quite possible that they are themselves unaware of how they process their information. So there is hardly any chance of us doing it for them.

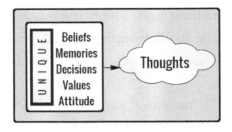

The Unconscious Program

It's not possible for us to accurately tell what other people are thinking or feeling. What we believe we know is just our perception of their perception. Which means two times the distortion!

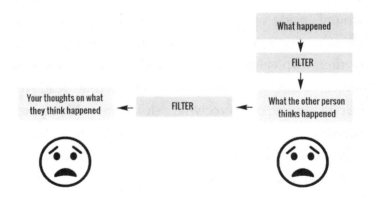

Mind reading is our perception of their perception

How do we Mind read?

What strategies do we unconsciously apply to guess what people are thinking or feeling? There are many ways although two of them are the most common. Broadly speaking, we either dip into our past experiences with them or assume that they think like us. Let's look at both of these possibilities.

Landscape of Experience

Based on your interpretations of your past experiences with certain people you predict their behavior in present situations. If you met someone who seemed temperamental the first time, you might use that judgment to predict her future behavior as well. Maybe the first time you met her, she was going through a difficult phase and is otherwise not temperamental.

Mind reading happens based on the file you select from your landscape of experience with a person and how you choose to interpret that file during storage as well as retrieval.

You might assume things, like the current situation is identical to the last one or that the person has not changed over time. This is one way we read people's minds.

Projection of Thoughts

Another way we read minds is by projecting our own thoughts and feelings onto others. Suppose I don't enjoy watching a game of cricket and you are a cricket fan. One day I enter the living room and see you watching a match and say to you, "Oh, I'm so sorry you have to watch this match because nothing interesting is being telecast." You will naturally be surprised because I have completely missed the fact that you *do* enjoy watching cricket. It's not something you *have to* watch. Now for a good question— who would have watched a cricket match if nothing else was being telecast? I guess that would be *me*!

Our thoughts form the basis for what we think another person might be thinking in a given situation. You might have observed this in your life as well. When somebody makes an opinion on your behalf which is way off the mark, you either correct the person or bite your tongue as clarifying seems inconsequential. Either way, you feel misunderstood.

This is how misunderstanding pans out. We might think that if we say or do a certain thing, the person in question will feel appreciated. Unfortunately, our gesture backfires and the person now feels undervalued, leaving us confused. We have projected what we like or dislike onto him assuming he is like us, although this might not be the case.

The concept of mind reading helps us appreciate that we don't always know what another person is thinking about us. What we fear could just be our imagination of their perception.

Why do we Mind read?

Our Discomfort with Incomplete Stories

Has it happened sometime with you that you lost something and simply could not stop searching for it even though you were getting late for another event on your schedule? Or you checked your phone incessantly waiting for a response to a message although you were very busy at that point in time? What we don't know grabs our attention especially when something important is at stake. We need to complete our stories, at least inside our minds, otherwise they continue to loop and sap our energy.

Now imagine the number of incomplete loops that you carry around inside yourself given that you are interacting with several people in your day-to-day life. Why did your teammate not return your call? Why did your friend change over time? Why were you not consulted in an important decision? It's impossible to know what each person is thinking in every given situation.

When the stakes are high the obsession with wanting to know the views of others is more as well. We could run the extra mile to gain clarity—check with other people concerned if they know any better, ask leading questions to make interpretations or become keenly observant of what's happening —*anything* that gives us some relief from not knowing.

Our mind struggles to give meaning to things, as without these cues, we won't know how to operate in this world. If I don't know whether someone enjoys my company or not, I will not know if I should make that call or not. If I don't know what my boss appreciates, I will not know how to act in order to get that promotion.

I might not be able to walk up to every person and ask, "Hey, I have my doubts about whether you like my company enough to hang out with me some-time," but the deep-seated need to know still exists. So, what now? Our mind, which is so good at creative writing jumps to our rescue and says, *"Don't worry, I got this*! I think this person doesn't like you because last time he saw you, he did not smile at you. Your boss likes it when you send him emails every day because that way he knows you are working hard. That is most likely the reason why he might give someone a promotion." You might not have any evidence to back your claims but now you have found a way to make sense of the things happening around you. These interpretations are mind reads which could be due to the projection of your thoughts.

Curbing of projections is a very important skill to have, more so if you are working as a coach or counselor. As a coach, I need to be aware of how much of what I interpret is the client's side of the story and how much is colored by my own beliefs and judgments because every client is unique (and is not me).

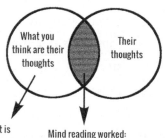

1) Deviation from what is
2) Imagination passed off as reality

Mind reading worked:
1) Based on past experiences or the similarity of your personalities, the projection on your thoughts worked
2) Your ability to accurately create the other person's worldview at your end

If we experience stress, disappointment or any other unresourceful state due to a mind read here is what we can do:

1. Ask the person: If it's really important to know what another person is thinking, the best way is to ask him/her. For instance, you can invite your manager for a meeting and say, "I am really interested in taking my skills to the next level. What qualities are you looking for in an ideal person suited for a promotion?" You might gain some insights that you might not have been able to guess. The manager could actually like the fact that you asked rather than assumed. This proactiveness could increase your chances of getting that promotion.

2. Make helpful interpretations: Suppose you cannot clarify things because you don't have access to the concerned person or you are unable to do so for some reason, you can consider making a positive interpretation of the situation. For example, you can tell yourself that the person who didn't smile at you was preoccupied and you can try initiating a conversation another time. This is not to delude ourselves into believing things that we like. It is to make interpretations that are in line with the outcomes we have chosen for ourselves. It will give us the strength required to take the necessary steps forward.

Ever since she lost her mother at an early age, Anna was raised with a lot of love and care by her father. She was very attached to him and ensured that she did not disappoint him in any way.

When she was 23 years old, her father decided to introduce her to his close friend's son who he thought was a suitable match for her. Anna agreed to meet him. They took a month to get to know each other. She liked some of his qualities but she didn't really fall in love with him. At least not enough to get married to him.

Anna knew that this alliance would make her father happy. When her father asked her about her decision, she hesitantly agreed. As soon as she consented, he looked happier than ever before. The date was fixed and the wedding preparations started.

As the wedding date approached, Anna began to feel a little anxious. She didn't believe that she was being true to her fiancée or her father. She approached her father on the day of the wedding and tried speaking her mind one last time but she couldn't. Her body was trembling and her voice betrayed her. The wedding was solemnized and she hoped to find love in her new-found husband.

The marriage didn't last a year. Anna and her husband went their separate ways due to temperamental differences. She regretted not speaking up about her feelings earlier. She wished she had said something and called off the wedding even on the day that it took place. She couldn't because she wondered:

"What will my fiancée think?"

"What will my father think?"

"What will all the guests at the wedding think?"

While all these were really good questions, they didn't lead up to a life that she liked. One that could give happiness to all people concerned.

One day she finally told her father about her apprehensions before marriage. He was shocked and said that he would have agreed to call off the wedding if only she had said so. Anna had assumed that he would not understand and contributed to what happened next.

There are situations in which mind reading can change the course of our lives. The first step is to be aware of what we are assuming and the next step is to clarify the assumptions especially when there is a lot at stake.

So what stops us, at times, from speaking our mind or clarifying things with others? Let's examine some of the underlying fears that cause us to give more weightage to what others think of us.

4

THE FEAR OF JUDGMENT

Has it happened sometime with you that you got on stage to give a speech and you got cold feet? You couldn't bear the thought of people watching you or listening to you. Fear of public speaking is frequently cited as one of the biggest fears that people experience. In my training programs, I have an exercise in which a participant from a group has to address the other participants. I have noticed a lot of discussion around who should represent the group. Many people seem to avoid going on stage. When I enquire about what stops them, I receive responses such as:

"I don't think I am good enough."

"I wonder what people will think of me."

"I'm sure people will make fun of me."

The underlying feeling in all these statements is the same—they fear being judged. I ask them if they have been judging me as a speaker during the program and they say, "No." I invite them to consider this:

Let's say that you are addressing an audience of about 50 people. Is it possible that *all* 50 are judging you? That would seem like a broad generalization to me. From my experience in public speaking, most people in the audience don't really judge me. They are merely considering my point of view.

Let's assume that a small percentage of people actually judge you. How useful would it be to base your competency as a speaker on the opinions of that handful of people? Would those people be able to stand up in front of an audience and speak as well as you? Even if they could, does that entitle them to judge another person who is making an attempt to do something that is considered difficult by most?

If everybody worried about their minority audience, the world would be devoid of great speakers. People would have drowned in anticipated judgment and would not have made any attempts whatsoever leaving us with a bare stage and a mic for no one to use. Even your favorite stand-up comedian faces the heat for his jokes from time to time. Don't you still want him to continue?

Instilling Shame

The fear of being judged makes people refrain from expressing their true feelings. The dots can often be joined back to childhood conditioning. Let's say a child is reprimanded for not conforming to certain deeply held family beliefs. This experience becomes even more distressing if it happens in the presence of other family members, relatives or friends. It could cause the child to fear the perception of people in the environment a lot more.

❧

Little Tara walks into the house while her parents are entertaining a guest, Aunt Lily. Tara is scolded by her mother for walking in with muddy shoes and not wishing her aunt. Her mother does not realize that instilling shame is rarely a positive way to condition any new behavior.

Tara is feeling slightly humiliated but she conceals it with a smile. She wishes her aunt, goes to her room and changes. She concludes that what her aunt thinks about her is more important than how she feels about herself. The child is unaware of her mother's lack of competency in guiding her and thinks that she needs to work harder to fit into the family's image of *the perfect child*.

·&·

When Tara grows up her mother might not necessarily be around her but her beliefs will subconsciously play out into Tara's adulthood. She might give more importance to others' perceptions of her as that is her survival mechanism. It gives her a sense of acceptance and okayness.

Fear of Success

When people begin to see success in the form of money, position or fame, they usually also see a change in their relationship dynamics. If they fear the judgment of others, at times, they feel scared to pursue their dreams as that might invoke the insecurities of the people around them. Subconsciously, they are aware of the unwanted changes that success can bring to their life. This knowledge prevents them from working on their goals. In other words, they fear being successful.

·&·

Jim was close to a few of his colleagues at work. They would sit in adjacent cubicles and catch up over coffee. They would spend evenings chatting at the cafeteria. One day, Jim got promoted and his workspace shifted to a cabin. He wasn't able to see his friends anymore. He occasionally walked down the hallway to meet them but that ate into his time. He had more responsibilities now and most of the coffee drinking happened over meetings. He wasn't able to meet his friends in the evening either. He did miss them but couldn't do much as he was himself under a lot of pressure.

Jim's friends started observing this natural distance that was created between them after his promotion. Some understood that he had become busy. Yet, the thought of their close friend spending long hours away from them led to resentment. Some others in the group thought to themselves that they never really wanted a promotion as they would end up losing their friends! This is how the fear of being successful results in self-sabotage.

❧

Fear of success is a little harder for an individual to detect in himself as it happens at a deeply unconscious level. If we identify with this fear, it helps to be empathetic towards the insecurities of others and wholeheartedly strive towards achieving our goals anyway. As we begin to see more success, we will find this fear gradually diminishing away.

We can not fix problems that are not ours to fix. If we restrict our results, it's not like we will suddenly fit in and be accepted. People will find other things they don't like about us if they choose to do so. Hence, regardless of the changes that success could bring, we can give ourselves the freedom to move towards excellence and enjoy new experiences.

The Spotlight Effect

Have you noticed that sometimes when you walk into a party, you feel like everyone is looking at you? When they talk to each other while smiling at you, you feel like they are talking about you. We do not have accurate information on what might be happening and could tend to assume it's about us.

Imagining that people notice us more than they actually do makes us feel like we are in the spotlight. This is referred to as the *spotlight effect*. It stems from the fear of social judgment. It is another example of a mind read which happens due to the projection of our thoughts. Since we are important to ourselves and spend a lot of time thinking about ourselves, we could assume that others are doing the same.

Has it happened sometime with you that you were ridiculed by someone in a meeting? Later, you checked with your colleague who was with you at the meeting about whether she noticed how you were treated. To your surprise, you realize that she didn't notice anything. This is because she was in her own bubble like most other people in the room. You felt like you were in the spotlight while people went about their own lives oblivious to what happened to you.

You have an aura around you which is a reflection of your energy field. It is strengthened or weakened by the emotions you are experiencing at any given point in time. You will have a powerful energy field around you when you are in a bright, positive, bounce-in-your step kind of mood. Similarly, a drain in your energy field can be felt when you are feeling anxious, angry or sad.

Just like you, other people have their own bubbles driven by their energy fields. They feel anxious, elated or something else based on their current set of conditions. They don't have the mind space to expand out of their bubble and think about you. Even if they occasionally do so to gossip about you or to go over their genuine concern for you, they will quickly return to their bubbles as that is a priority for them. They are invariably more invested in themselves unless they believe that you rocked their boat in some way.

Most of what happens in the world has nothing to do with you.

5

RECLAIMING YOUR SPACE

We don't care for the views of certain people in our life. Maybe because their views are not relevant to us or we find them to be pushy with respect to giving us their opinions. It helps to equip ourselves with ways to deal with them so that we can focus our limited energy on things that matter to us.

Unsolicited Advice

We have all met a person who freely gave us advice on how we should think, act or feel in given situations. Do you remember how it felt particularly if you were not looking for it? Unsolicited advice is mostly self-serving and assumes that the person giving it is in some way more qualified and knowledgeable than the listener.

Regardless of whether one has a positive intention or not, giving unsolicited advice is not helpful. As we saw earlier, identity impacts the weightage given to a person's opinion. People who routinely give unsolicited advice will, unfortunately, be branded as such and others will not take what they have to say seriously. Eventually, people will stop giving them attention and they will not be in a position to influence anyone.

If you are at the receiving end of such advice, you can pause for a moment and see if there is any merit in what is being said. Separate the signal from the noise. If you feel like there is nothing in it for you and someone is overstepping your boundaries, it's ok to say so because nodding along is equivalent to asking for more. You can thank them and let them know that you already have a plan for yourself and are not looking for any new ideas or suggestions. This needs to be done with care because the intention is to reclaim your space, not to hurt them.

Dealing with Difficult People

People who are in a habit of judging others will do the same with you, with little or no motivation. They will get hurt just by your presence, even if you say or do nothing. The negative suggestions given to you by them are to make you think, act and feel as they want you to. They usually come from a space of entitlement. They will not be happy with you no matter what you do. It is like pouring water into a bucket that has a hole at the bottom. How much effort are you willing to put in before you get exhausted and realize that understanding their perspective, adapting accordingly or sacrificing your happiness will not get you the intended result? It can be quite disheartening because there is no way to fill this bucket.

Adapting beyond a certain point could make people take you for granted. They will not be able to value your efforts to adapt. When you do not stand up for yourself, they could lose respect for you because they see you as an *easy* person. Others create impressions about you the way you do about them. Hence, the amount you endure will decide what kind of behavior you can expect from them in the future.

Giving a person's views weightage because they will become angry with you, punish you or leave you amounts to manipulation.

In this case, you care for what they want out of fear. You don't want to be put through the misery that they are capable of inflicting on you. You adapt and they notice that their methods are working. Once they register what works, they will use that to get you to comply.

If you see somebody habitually using methods to instill a sense of fear in you, realize one thing for sure—they are more scared from inside than you are! Sounds a little counter-intuitive but that is what it usually is. Control freaks are controlling out of fear of something that might happen if they stopped controlling, an after-effect that they might not be able to handle.

If you are an empathetic person it is going to be even more difficult for you. People who expect a lot from others and take the liberty to mistreat them if they fall short usually prefer empathetic people—ones who really care for their views. An evaluation will need to be done in this case. Can we set a boundary with the person so we get some space?

Setting Boundaries

Setting boundaries is about telling people what works for you and what doesn't. You also state what they can expect from you if your boundaries are violated. Once you define a boundary you have to execute what you said you would do if they violated it. If you fail to do so, your boundaries will not hold any value and will be perceived as *empty threats*.

Setting boundaries can be a bit challenging, especially if you are dealing with difficult people. They will lash out at you for having your own views. They can not stand the fact that you are your own person and not what they want you to be.

If a person gets mad at you for setting a boundary, it is a big indicator that a boundary was required in the first place.

They don't like boundaries because it makes them feel like they can't control you anymore. Lack of control makes them anxious and now they will do *anything* to make the equation to go back to the way it was—being extra nice to you, fulfilling your needs before you state them, shouting at you or threatening to break off with you.

When they try everything and nothing works they will get tired in a while. Some of them will walk away but here is the surprising part—a majority of them will stay! They realize subconsciously that they have been contributing to the situation. The supply of care and attention you are giving them is hard to get elsewhere. You are seen as short supply and suddenly the anxiety of you getting away is too much for them to handle. Their anxiety drives them to treat you in different ways—from very nice to very harsh and other intermediate shades in the continuum of possible treatments.

If you have ever dealt with a controlling person you know how draining it can be. Getting space from such a person is easy at times. Let's say it's a friend whom you meet once in a way. It's easy to reduce the frequency of interactions and not be too bothered by it. However, if it's your boss with whom you have to work or your partner with whom you live, it might be harder to distance yourself. In this case, you will need special skills to cope with the situation—to establish boundaries, to reinforce boundaries and to take care of yourself when you receive pushback for asserting yourself. We will go over ways to gain these skills in *7 Best Practices to Stop Worrying About Others.*

The Pain-Pleasure Equation

Adjusting with others is inevitable although we need to be aware of how much of what we are willing to put up with. When communicating our needs, setting boundaries or standing up for ourselves don't work, we experience despair. The decision of staying in the relationship primarily depends on the pain-pleasure equation.

The definitions of *pain* and *pleasure* are subjective to each person. What is pain to one may be pleasure to another and vice versa. This subjective experience decides the future of the relationship. If the pain you get by being in a relationship is more than the pleasure, you will want out of it. If the pleasure you get by being in a relationship outweighs the pain of being in it, then you will stay.

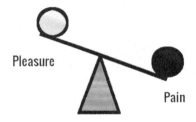

We leave when the pain of being in a relationship exceeds the pleasure we get out of it

Pleasure

Pain

Let's think of a loving couple who nurture each other during difficult times. Occasionally they quarrel but they invariably make up. They laugh at their life situations and soon forget about everything that happened. The reconciliation was possible because the good times they shared outweighed their difficult times. If their quarrels and disagreements were to become more than their happy moments together, we can expect them to drift apart. So the survival of the relationship depends on whether the two people spend more time in the pleasure zone or the pain one.

When a person wants out of a relationship, things can become difficult. Anticipated problems can cause some people to continue being in their relationships half-heartedly. I hear reasons for it such as:

"They have done so much for me so I should stay with them."

"Once upon a time we were so happy together so I should keep this relationship going."

There are people who have done a lot for us. They are wonderful and good at heart. At the same time when the relationship becomes distressing and for some reason, we are unable to find the same happiness we used to with them, it's time to reconsider what we want to do going forward. We don't want to undermine what they have done for us. It's just that when we use the *once-upon-a-time happiness* as a reason to put up with things we don't like, we live a compromised life, which results in frustration.

The first option in this case is always self-work. To see if there is something we can do to understand the person's perspective and improve the relationship. However, when our attempts fail we might have to move away from a relationship that drains our system physically or mentally.

It doesn't really matter what caused two people to drift apart. Sometimes people change or they might have been a certain way all along and over time we discovered their true personalities. We have all been in relationships where things were awesome initially and fizzled out later or were rough initially and became smooth later. Getting to know a person is like peeling away the layers of an onion. You don't know what you are going to discover but when you do, you may or may not like it.

Pulling the plug on a relationship is not easy. Feelings are going to be hurt. Even when people want out of a relationship, if the other person rejects them first, they feel hurt. Somehow the concept of someone not liking us is hard for us to accept.

6

GROUPS: DO YOU FIT IN OR STAND OUT?

Societies, groups and communities have rules by which they like their members to abide. These rules are usually unstated and ambiguous. They vary from one place and culture to another. We don't have a handbook that spells things out for us.

It helps society to have you follow their norms. People who conform to those rules *fit in* and those who don't *stand out*. Societal control is exerted by being different with those who stand out. This demotivates people from doing so as they will have to pay the price for it. Having a positive public opinion is important to people which makes them usually fall in line.

At an early age, we observe people in our environment judging others which makes us implicitly conclude that we will be judged as well if we were like the *misfits* in question. So, it's in our best interest to do what everyone else is doing in order to be liked and accepted.

Social proof is a way of limiting one's life—making it identical, without reason, to everyone else's. It does not appreciate the fact that each one of us is unique and will want different things for ourselves.

If your decisions don't hurt people or violate boundaries and just design a life you want for yourself then here is one possible line of action—go over the pros and cons with people who matter, consider how your decision impacts your ecology and do what works best for you because you know that it's difficult to satisfy everybody.

When your decisions cause you to break out of the mold, people might not know how to respond to you. Some people will appreciate that you are different while others might ridicule you. Either way, there is no right or wrong answer. The best way to get some clarity is to mentally fast forward your life by ten years and visualize how you would like it to look. Would you regret not doing something you could do today?

Self-Image vs. Public Image

If someone were to praise you for your good looks or great achievements would you question their opinions? You might not because it feels good.

Our public image often drives our self-image and the other way round. Both are important to us. The extent to which the two images are coupled varies from person to person.

External referenced people look for validation on the outside. They know they are ok if other people think so. Public opinion is more important to them than their own opinion. For example, a person thinks she looks good *only* if her friends say so and not otherwise.

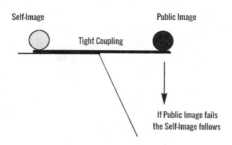

The coupling between the Public Image and Self-Image is tight

They feel successful when people appreciate them and feel like they have failed when people don't. This is due to the strong coupling between their two images.

Internal referenced people look for validation on the inside. Their sense of success and failure comes from their own set of parameters that they have created for themselves. Public opinion will matter to them but not as much as their own. For example, a person is greatly appreciated by his team for a presentation he created for a meeting. However, he isn't happy with the presentation as he thinks it was not up to the mark.

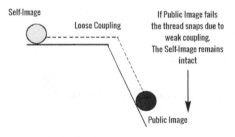

The coupling between the Public Image and Self-Image is loose

An internal referenced person will also feel the effects of what people are saying about him/her.

However, these feelings will be less intense owing to the weak coupling between the two images.

Praise -> The person will believe and rise.

Criticism -> The person will believe and fall.

The tighter the coupling between self-image and public image, the greater the strength of the resultant belief.

ॐ

In March 2016, I attended a training program conducted by an esteemed mental health institution in my city. Midway through the program, I realized that I was the only person in the room who wasn't a doctor. I came from a coaching and training background while the others were graduates from medical colleges. Sometimes they used jargon that flew right past me. I would clarify my doubts whenever I got an opportunity. The other participants figured out that I was not one among them. I could only hope that my questions didn't interrupt their learning process in some way.

When the session was advertised it was open to all and so I attended it. In my opinion, no training goes waste. There is always scope to learn more, with doctors or otherwise. Worrying about what people will think about who I am and how much I know would have prevented me from picking up some of the finest skills from experienced teachers.

By the end of the program, I made a bunch of friends and was satisfied with the week's work. I doubt any of that would have been possible if I had thought to myself, "It's better I don't ask questions and reveal my amateur status. What will these participants think of me?"

If I disguise my lack of knowledge, it will ensure I learn nothing more than what I already know. Amateurs are not born amateurs. Every master was once an amateur, including the trainer who stands on the dias and teaches us.

Today when I conduct training programs I don't allow participants to call any of their questions basic or silly. A doubt needs clarification, not judgment.

Social Media Influence

There was a time when photographs were not available digitally. In my childhood days, I remember us sharing pictures with family and friends by actually printing them out and snail mailing them. Did we know if the recipients liked the pictures or not? Not really.

Today the idea of doing something like that is absurd. Everything happens at a lightning-fast pace. We can click a picture, share it with thousands of people and instantly see their reaction to it. We can share every moment of our lives—what we eat, where we go or whom we meet in a matter of seconds. Social media has its advantages in terms of knowing what is happening with people and keeping in touch with their lives. However, it is a double-edged sword that needs to be used with caution.

Constant messages from social media channels serve as a gentle reminder to the fact that we are surrounded by public opinions. Today, people are well-informed about what is happening with others. You might have noticed some time that news about you traveled really fast even when you did not share it. That is how powerful a self-run media channel is.

Often emotions get linked to social media posts. When people get *likes* and *shares* on their posts they feel like they are being liked as people which results in a surge of good feelings. The effect lasts for a moment and soon they want more. They could get addicted to that feeling of being appreciated even though they don't know if it's true appreciation or just a passing click of a button.

When self-image strongly depends on public image, people give importance to others' perceptions of them. The idea of people *liking* them or *following* them can be quite gratifying. When nobody responds to their posts they could feel rejected. People find it stressful to manage their online personas once their emotions get attached to them.

It helps to periodically evaluate the usefulness of our social media channels and their impact on us. If the coupling between our self-image and public image is loose, we can get away with feeling comfortable with ourselves even if people don't respond positively to what we publish. That way we can continue to use the social media channels for the benefit they provide and stay clear of any unwanted effects on us.

We will go over ways to loosen the coupling between our self-image and public image in *7 Best Practices to Stop Worrying About Others*. In the upcoming sections, we will examine different scenarios in which our concern for how other people perceive us could affect the quality of our life.

7

PERCEPTIONS IN ROMANTIC RELATIONSHIPS

Ted was one of the most popular guys in college. Being the head of the college cultural team kept him in the limelight. Many girls in college wanted to go out with him. However, Ted was not interested in the girls who gave him attention. He had his eyes set on Nancy, one of the shy girls in class. He couldn't bring himself to tell her how he felt out of fear of being rejected. He imagined that she would laugh at him. The thought of that happening was enough to kill him.

Time went by. Both Ted and Nancy graduated from college and moved on with their lives. They settled down with different people and lost touch. Ten years later, Nancy is happy with her marriage. However, Ted's marriage didn't work out.

As luck would have it, Ted and Nancy met again at a college friend Mike's party. When Ted saw Nancy he was suddenly transported back to college—he remembered how much he adored her, how he couldn't express himself and the disappointment he faced when he realized that he might never see her again. A giant wave from the past splashed on him.

After the party got over Ted asked Mike about Nancy. He wanted to know about where she had been all these years. Mike gave him the details. He added that back in college Nancy really liked Ted but since he didn't show any interest, she had moved on.

✦

As a coach, I frequently come across such stories. People keep their feelings to themselves out of fear of how they will be perceived if they were to express themselves. They get into a habit of hiding their feelings to a point where they don't know how they are feeling. Another person doesn't stand a chance at deciphering.

I don't mean to imply that if Ted had asked Nancy out their relationship would have definitely worked out well. We are just looking for ways of expressing ourselves that will reduce the randomness we experience in our lives and get us more of what we want.

I agree that we can not be vulnerable with everybody. There could be people who don't understand us, who could expose us to the world or who could hurt us with their response. We all have been in situations where we trusted someone too quickly only to get judged or rejected in the process. However, if these people prevent us from taking our chances it could result in a limited life. We could be deprived of all those experiences that we could have had if only we had the courage to ask for what we wanted without worrying about what others would think.

Entering a Relationship

Romantic relationships operate in a paradigm of their own. Loving someone makes a person undergo the risk of being hurt. As feelings become intense so does the vulnerability. This is one of the reasons why people feel unsure about whether they should express their feelings to the person concerned or not. If they imagine that their feelings will not be reciprocated, there are some subsequent scenarios that they usually fear:

1. Anticipated pain they will go through due to perceived rejection by *the one*.
2. The fear of how their public image will be affected if others get to know of their feelings.
3. The fear of spoiling *what is*. If the relationship is currently based on friendship and now there is an attempt to make it something more, it might jeopardize the existing relationship. Once the feelings are out in the open, the recipient of the message might leave the scene if things become awkward. This causes confusion over the status of the relationship.

These fears prevent people from taking the first step.

If you are in a similar situation and you decide to tell the person how you feel (for the sake of simplicity we assume that you and the person in question are not attached to anyone else), there is a chance that he/she might accept that giving yourselves an opportunity to get to know each other is a good idea.

On the other hand, if things don't happen as per what you hoped for, you still have clarity about where you stand. So much better than going through life wondering what might have been. If you are bothered about how you will be perceived in this situation, it helps to remember that most people have themselves gone through a heartbreak at least once and in all probability, they know how it feels. Also, if people are not understanding of the situation or make fun of you for it (including the one you love), they probably weren't the type of people whom you wanted to be with anyway. You deserve people who are empathetic towards your feelings even if they don't reciprocate it.

We are not trying to set a rule—speak up or hold back. We just want to make a decision that we will appreciate down the road. One that is more in line with what we want.

So check with yourself:

1. Is it possible that, at a later point in time, you will regret not expressing your feelings?
2. Would you be able to love yourself even if your feelings were not reciprocated?
3. How important is it to you what other people think about you?
4. Is there any tangible impact of their views on your life?

Leaving a Relationship

When I hear clients in coaching sessions say they want out of a romantic relationship the first concern that usually comes up for them is about the thoughts and feelings of the person they are going to break off with. Then, at times, they are worried about what people in their social circle might think of the relationship that has ended.

Let's look at Fred who is considering opting out of a relationship with Tracy that lasted two years. He is struggling with an internal dialogue of what will happen if Tracy never recovers from the separation. His questions are:

"Will she be ok?"

"Am I doing the wrong thing by wanting to break off?"

"Can I live with the guilt of hurting someone who is good?"

When people want to part ways, it's not always about one person being *bad* or *wrong*. It's just that those two people were not right for each other. They wanted different things from life. They couldn't see themselves committed to each other for various reasons. In the case mentioned above, Fred wanted out as he thought Tracy wasn't the person he assumed she was when they started off. He cares for her feelings but doesn't want to be in a relationship with her.

People who continue to be in a relationship when they don't want to are doing a disservice to all—the ones they are with, the ones those people could be with and above all themselves. It's impossible to love anyone forcibly and the effort of trying to keep someone happy without being happy oneself is pointless. You can pretend to like someone for some time but you can not sustain the act over a period of time.

If repeated attempts to make things work fail and you really want out, you might have to let the person know how you feel. The person at the receiving end will most likely feel disappointed. Yet, the foundation for your current as well as future relationships will be based on authentic feelings (not what you are *supposed* to feel). Expressing your true self is good, not only for yourself but for your partner as well, even if it causes some discomfort temporarily.

Public opinion on a breakup depends on the extent to which the two people involved had announced their relationship status to the world. If they were engaged or married and they called it off, it could draw more attention than if not many people were aware of it.

We might like a line between our public lives and personal lives. Unfortunately, that might not always be possible. If there is a concern about other people in the world and their thoughts on your breakup, I would like to emphasize that no one is going to live your life for you even for a day. The people who talk about you will very soon forget about you and get busy talking about someone else. Some people might be genuinely concerned about you and yet, your decisions will have more implications for you than anybody else. The focus needs to be on what works best for you and your partner.

8

WORK LIFE HAPPINESS QUOTIENT

The environment in which we work becomes our mini-universe. Most people spend more time at their workplace than at home. The workplace ecosystem is very different from the friends and family one to which you might be emotionally attached. Yet, your relationship with co-workers and their opinions about you are important. There will be seniors who will appraise you as a result of which you could get promoted or receive certain benefits that can improve your overall *work life happiness quotient*. The cooperation of your subordinates is required to deliver what you promised as a team. A healthy give and take with your peers can help you grow in the organization. People create impressions about you that will decide the level of cooperation you will receive from them in the future. Hence, the image you have created for yourself is important.

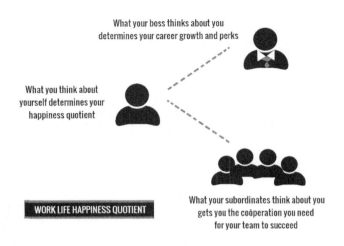

What your boss thinks about you determines your career growth and perks

What you think about yourself determines your happiness quotient

WORK LIFE HAPPINESS QUOTIENT

What your subordinates think about you gets you the coöperation you need for your team to succeed

At every level, you could experience pressure from different directions. Performance pressure based on the expectations from your managers, peer pressure based on how people at your level are performing and the stress of managing your subordinates who may or may not be working as per your expectation. If you have a difficult boss, most of your energy will be expended in keeping things civil. You could feel like you are walking on a landmine where your patience is tested at every step. If you are very good at your job, you could have to deal with the envy and insecurities of co-workers.

Dealing with this much pressure requires a frame of mind in which you do your job and don't care too much about others. At the same time, like we saw, what others think about us is important. We need to strike a balance, as always. If you are a working professional, here are a few ways in which you can manage your workplace persona:

1. Develop an identity. In the first chapter of the book, we saw that identity decides the weightage we give to a person's opinions. In order to be influential, you need to develop an identity in the worlds of your co-workers. One way to do that is to genuinely try to understand their needs. If they see you as a person who cares for them, the chances of their cooperating with you become high. This will require effort and time on your part but will pay dividends in the long run.

2. Have consistent behavior with people across levels in the organization and clients as well. Companies have formal training for better behavior and presentation of oneself to clients. Likewise, some people have a better tonality reserved for seniors in a company as opposed to subordinates. It helps to have a consistently good attitude towards people at all levels. It not only gets ingrained into your personality but also incorporated in your image, which helps in further establishing your identity. Haven't we seen someone who is extremely well behaved with the supervisor and in an instant turns around and snaps at his subordinate? This behavior results

in confusion in the observer's mind as to which one of these two personalities is actually true.

3. Give people opportunities to tell you what they are thinking by scheduling downtime on a regular basis. Very often in business coaching sessions, I have found that people are not able to express their views simply because they don't have the right opportunity to do so. If everybody is working towards strict deadlines and holding up tight schedules, there is no time to talk about what's bothering them or what could get them better results. It's like driving a car around with no fuel and saying that we don't have the time to fill it. It's eventually going to break down anyway.

4. Clearly state your boundaries and reinforce them as and when necessary. People treat you only in the way that you allow them to. If your cordial conduct is being taken for granted or if people are not aware of what you want, you need to take action. For instance, you might need to tell your manager that you can not take up more work as you are overloaded with your current assignments or you might have to tell your subordinates that if they fail to deliver one more time, you will have to take away some of their perks. Regular coaching makes this process easier. I have seen clients in my business coaching sessions who went from not being able to

say anything to setting healthy boundaries with their colleagues in a matter of a few weeks.

5. Develop skills to deal with difficult co-workers. The ones who don't like you could make life difficult for you on a daily basis. If setting boundaries doesn't work, you just need to find a way to co-exist. There is not much benefit in spending time thinking about their temperaments. It is like trying to solve their personality-related problems which need self-work and commitment on their part. You can not wish their feelings away either. Let's say you tried to understand their perspective, you asked them for what you need and even tried your best to give them what they need. If that brings no result, just play along, keep things transactional and get the work done. While you maintain decorum and accomplish things the *getting together* part might eventually work out.

Your work life happiness quotient is directly proportionate to your relationship with your colleagues. The methods mentioned above can help in improving interpersonal relationships which will, in turn, support you in fulfilling your aspirations.

9

STUDENT LIFE HAPPINESS QUOTIENT

Managing one's image at an educational institution is stressful for students because their minds are still in the developmental stage. Students are increasingly coming under the pressure of securing marks, ranks and positions that give them social status in their institutions. They experience peer pressure by comparing themselves to other students in their class. They watch the class toppers get recognition at school events for their achievements.

Sometimes the recognition is not done out loud and yet it gets subtly conveyed to students through the attitude of people towards them. These experiences can significantly impact students during their growing up years as they are in the process of building their self-image by imbibing the views that they receive from their environment.

When the focus of students shifts to what others think of them and they start to work hard to gain the approval of teachers and admiration of peers, the very reason behind joining an educational institution gets defeated. Learning is no longer the agenda, outdoing is. Later when they step into the world they are taught about the importance of teamwork. It is difficult for them as all through their developmental years they were trying to get ahead of everyone else. They wanted to get more marks than others and a better rank so that they could get that coveted seat in the university. Today, we want them to think differently and focus on achieving goals as a team. They will need time and effort to revise their thinking, if at all they choose to do so.

Pete was the captain of the school basketball team. He was thrilled as his team had won the inter-school basketball competition that year. His close friend Mike was doing well academically. He was given the *Student of the Year* award for securing the highest marks in the final exams. Both friends were delighted with their achievements. Their names were announced in the school assembly and they were awarded medals for the same.

Unfortunately, the next year didn't turn out so well for either of them. Pete got dropped out of the basketball team and a newcomer was taken in. Mike also slipped to the second position as someone marginally outdid him in the final exam. This year different people received the awards. Pete and Mike felt lost at the award ceremony as the school got busy congratulating the next set of winners. They decided to speak to their school counselor about it.

During their individual sessions, they both realized something very similar. Pete played basketball for the love of the game. He could continue enjoying it even if he wasn't a part of the school team. His past achievements helped him build a great public image but how much of that did he personally want for himself?

Mike also realized that he had been pressurizing himself to rank first in class to maintain the *Student of the Year* status he enjoyed so much. If he could focus on his own reasons for studying, he could continue to learn as much he wanted without caring about the resultant social status.

☙

It is good to recognize students who perform well. We all love recognition when we achieve something, don't we? However, what works best is to continuously instill a sense of worthiness in all children by allowing them to connect with their special qualities.

A child's self-image is dependent on the public image especially during the formative years and hence more care needs to be taken to ensure that the environment nurtures both the images of the budding mind. One way to do this is to appreciate each child for what he/she is and then provide encouragement to be more. Putting a few up on a pedestal might not only make others believe that they lack in some way but could also pressurize the ones who are up there.

10

WAYS TO RECLAIM YOUR POWER

Following some simple methods can help you reclaim your power and take decisions easily. Once you put these methods into practice you will notice being more in control of situations. You will also experience increased happiness and contentment on a day-to-day basis.

Follow Your Passion

Doing what you are passionate about is a great way to increase your happiness quotient. Don't we feel fully alive when we do things that we absolutely love?

When you decide to follow your dreams or do something you are passionate about, initially people might reject your views and you could face some resistance. Two reasons why this usually happens are:

1) **Injected Self-Doubt from others**: People project their self-doubts onto you which could make you doubt yourself as well.

2) **Comfort Zone Resistance**: They don't doubt your success but do not want to come out of their comfort zone, which they will have to, since you changed the equation.

Let us look into each of these reasons in greater detail.

1. Injected Self-Doubt from others

Have you ever tried telling another person about your dream project? Do you remember how excited you were? How was the reaction of the person you were telling this to? You might have noticed that it is rare to find someone as excited as you are about your dreams. People feel discouraged when others around them don't share their excitement. Sometimes it goes one step beyond. They are told that their goals are not worth pursuing or that they will not succeed. This injects fear in their minds which prevents them from taking the first step.

What would you do if you were not afraid?

The people who perceive your vision operate out of their limited set of experiences. They might not know what your dreams mean to you or how successful you could be if only you gave yourself a chance. Their world view says, "Bad idea. You can't do this!"

Their limiting beliefs could be created by their own unsuccessful attempts at doing something or their observation of others who could not achieve their goals. This observation leads to the conclusion that others, including you, might be unsuccessful as well. Their generalization of situations goes unchallenged. They might believe that they are protecting you from a disappointing result. One that has already happened in their minds.

They may or may not want to challenge their own limiting beliefs but you can. Don't let anybody tell you what you can or what you can't do. When people say, *"You can't do it"* what they actually mean is that *they* can't do it.

How does anybody know what you can and what you can't do?

So, when you get some discouraging advice here are some things to check:

- Does this person really know a lot more about the given field than you do?
- Has this person taken the time and effort to understand you as a person?
- Has this person strived out of his/her comfort zone to achieve any goals?

If the answer to the above questions is *'no'* then you can accordingly assign a value to the incoming suggestion and take your decision. On the other hand, if the answers are *'yes'* then you might need to consider what is being said to you.

We don't mean to follow our dreams without careful evaluation of the risks involved. Understanding the implications of our decisions on our family, health and finances is as important as doing what we like. We do not want to end up in financial difficulties because we just did whatever our hearts told us to do.

When we encourage ourselves to follow our dreams, it is only the first step towards figuring out a way to meet other needs that co-exist in our life like having great relationships, health, fitness and finances. We don't want to jeopardize any one aspect while pursuing another. At the same time, we want to give ourselves the opportunity of doing what we like, whether professionally or as a hobby.

We have chosen our dreams and our dreams have also chosen us. If we don't do what we really love we will continue to nurse that desire inside of us, one that will ferment because it didn't find an outlet to express itself.

2. Comfort Zone Resistance

People love their comfort zone. They like to stay there and would like you to stay in yours too. As you step out of your comfort zone, they will have to do the same in order to adapt. Otherwise, they won't know how to relate to you anymore.

❧

Susan quit her job as a graphic designer and became a stay-at-home mother. Her family had the comfort of having a person available round the clock who tended to their needs. Five years later, she felt like her children were old enough to take care of themselves. She decided to get back to work. She started her own company which provided graphic design services.

Her family didn't like the idea very much as they preferred her to be around more often. She decided to work on her dream project anyway. Her hours away from home made them resentful. They didn't like the fact that their breakfast was kept on the table and preferred being served with a hot cup of tea. They didn't like the extra effort they had to put into procuring things for the house and keeping it clean. As Susan stepped out of her comfort zone, the rest of the family had no choice but to do the same.

In a matter of time, things settled down for everyone. Susan found ways to be around at home more often. She managed to balance her work and personal life better. Her family was also empowered to do their own work and were not as dependent on her as before. Susan pursued her dreams. She also cared for what her family needed to the best extent possible and kept going. This new-found balance helped her feel fulfilled in both fronts of her life.

Whatever you want and don't have lies just outside your comfort zone. You will experience growth as soon as you try to stretch out and get it. Patience is required while you are doing this as it takes time for changes to sink it. Not only for you but also the people in your environment.

Being at Ease with Yourself

Before seeking any kind of approval from others, it helps to examine how much we approve of ourselves. To understand this, all we need to do is examine our self-talk. If I do something and tell myself I should not have done it, I feel something and tell myself I shouldn't have felt so, I look at myself in the mirror and say that I shouldn't look that way, there is an underlying message in these thoughts—that I am not ok the way I am.

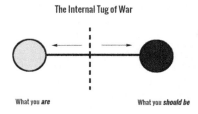

The Internal Tug of War

What you *are*　　　　What you *should be*

Bridging the gap between what you *are* and what you believe you *should be* can be difficult, at least in the moment. It results in discomfort and dissatisfaction with *what is*.

Every time you tell yourself that you should be something else, you rob yourself of who you are. You have special qualities that you might not spend time thinking about. You have already benefited from those qualities as there are people who love you for it.

An unconditional acceptance of who you are can free you up from spending a lot of energy tussling with who you are not. That does not mean to say that we will never aim at being anything more. It just means that to be where we want to be requires us to start with where we are right now.

Fritz Perls, the founder of Gestalt therapy, gives us the example of a mountain climber. When the climber sets his first foot firmly it becomes possible for him to climb up with his next foot. Without the first foot being secure he will fall down. So we begin with complete acceptance of ourselves first and then go beyond.

When people make you feel like you're not enough, it could be their own missing self-love that's being projected onto you. We have already seen how projections work. Now let's look at its implication in this case.

People who don't feel it's ok to be themselves might not be ok if you are yourself. If they never felt like they were enough, whatever you do might not be enough. So you have a choice of loving and accepting yourself while looking for areas of improvement or accepting others' judgments of you as true and trying hard to be something you are not.

If people love you only if you change yourself for them, it will not be a sustainable model in the long run. Inevitably some time the mask will drop off revealing your true self. At this point in time, things will become even more complicated as people will reorient to their new discovery of you resulting in confusion. The relationship will start to deteriorate because you worked so hard to be something you're not and still no one's happy.

When we compromise on our identity, morals or values, our mental health gets compromised which leads to frustration and resentment. Hence, being yourself from the beginning and letting people decide whether they want to be with you or not is a helpful thing to do. It removes the uncertainty of what the future holds and increases the probability of finding more people who are good for you in the long run—the people who know you well and will like you anyway.

A Strong Foundation of Principles

We saw in the section on *Mind reading* that each one of us has a unique map that we use to understand the world. Our map is created by our life experiences and our interpretations of them. A useful map is one which matches well with what is happening in the outside world and can help us successfully navigate through it.

If, at every given opportunity, you have to decide whether something is good for you or not and make calculations based on millions of bits of incoming information, you will be too overwhelmed to decide anything effectively. The ease of decision-making is possible by having a set of principles that you stand by, no matter what.

❧

Adam and Ken are two teammates who report to their manager called Sam. Adam has a principle of treating people with unconditional positive regard. He doesn't stop to think if he would gain something from them or not. Ken, on the other hand, is also nice to people but prefers to treat his supervisors better than his subordinates.

When Ken realized that Sam was not in charge of the promotions in the upcoming year, he became cold towards him and started spending more time trying to impress other managers who he thought would get him the promotion. Adam had a good attitude towards Sam just as he had towards everyone else in the organization.

Finally, the day came that Ken was eagerly waiting for. The promotions were announced. Adam got promoted but unfortunately Ken did not. When he inquired about what happened he realized that the news of Sam not weighing in on the promotion was false. Apparently, Sam did have a role to play in deciding who goes to the next level.

Adam continued to have a good attitude towards Sam. He didn't change his behavior even after he got promoted. Ken was unable to challenge Sam as he knew that somewhere he had made a mistake. Sam was happy with his decision. Adam's principle, of giving unconditional regard, seemed much required at the next level.

Ken had to make additional decisions regarding whom to be nice to and how much. He faced the stress of making a wrong decision. People around him were confused because they did not know what to expect of him. Adam, on the other hand, was free from having to decide. He valued everybody irrespective of the position they worked at or what they could do for him. This gave him the freedom to focus on his work. His colleagues liked working with him too. There was a comfort in knowing what they could expect of him. It not only freed up Adam, it freed other people up as well.

᠁

Your principles do not go unnoticed. They speak volumes in the form of small decisions you take unconsciously every minute. What you stand for irrespective of what others are doing, saying or thinking will be picked up by people in a matter of time. Having a clearly defined set of principles is much required to successfully navigate through life because you know that if you don't stand for something you will fall for everything.

It is important to be observant of the results you are getting by following your principles. For instance, if a person says, "I have a principle based on which I give myself the permission to be harsh with people who make mistakes because that is the only way they will learn." We don't know how well following this principle serves the person in the long run.

Carefully examining which principles are getting you great results will give you an idea as to where you can invest more of your energy and which ones you need to re-examine.

Having principles doesn't always make your life easy. There will be times when you will be tested and when standing up for your principles could give you more problems to deal with than you ever wanted. Despite that, being aware of what's important to you and acting in accordance with it will give you peace and happiness in the long run.

People who do not have a strong set of principles and change according to situations or whatever is convenient end up feeling miserable. Their priorities are not set; their needs are unclear leading to overall instability and confusion.

Your Circle of Power

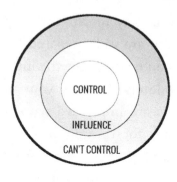

CIRCLE OF POWER

Your circle of control encompasses everything that is in your control like your thoughts, feelings and behaviors that result from it. For instance, you might be able to control your decision to stay in a job, start a business or be in a relationship.

Then there are people, situations, or circumstances that you can not control but can influence. Let's say you have a partner, personal or professional, who doesn't share your views on a certain decision. You can, however, influence the person into thinking on the lines that you want. These things encompass your circle of influence.

We also have situations that are neither in our control nor under our influence. These things are best not tussled with as they could tire us out without getting us any result. Let's say, you have a job interview. You are well prepared for it. Unfortunately, the day you have to give the interview you get sick and someone else is given your interview slot. The interviewers are impressed with that applicant and hire him/her for the job canceling all further interviews, including yours. You can't help but feel that if you had given the interview, you might have been selected.

Preparing for the interview was in your circle of control and the interviewers were in your circle of influence but falling sick was outside both these circles. It was not something you could control or influence. The more a person waddles in this zone, the greater is the feeling of helplessness. You might wish that you never fell sick or a person who is frustrated trying to change his partner might wish he never got involved with that person to begin with. It's common to fantasize about not having a problem and internally create an alternate reality that provides some temporary relief from what is. We know that it is not going to change the situation in any way. We just feel worse when we compare *what is* to *what could have been*. Hence, the things that are outside our control or influence are best left as they are.

When you control what's in your control, what's not in your control also starts to come into your control, thereby, expanding your circle of influence.

What other people think and feel about us is not in our control. We can not really *make* people think in a certain way. However, there are ways using which we can influence them without outrightly trying to do so.

If people sense that you are trying to influence them they will switch off. This happens especially when they are not looking for your views or they do not consider you to be an authority on the subject. Resistance to unwanted influence happens at an unconscious level and could cause the listener to perceive you as authoritative, dominating or controlling. This impression built over time could result in more damage to your relationship, thereby eliminating even slim chances of you influencing the person.

You can reclaim your power by expanding your circle of influence by focusing on what's inside your circle of control, that is, your own thoughts and feelings.

David asked his manager, Peter, for a promotion but was unfortunately turned down. David tried explaining to Peter multiple times that he was the perfect candidate for the promotion and was far better than his counterparts but in vain. David soon realized that his attempts to talk to Peter into promoting him were not working. So he decided to do something different.

He stopped talking to Peter about the promotion altogether. He started focussing on being very efficient in the tasks that were assigned to him. He trained himself in the areas where he needed to improve his skills and equipped himself with the necessary knowledge to do his tasks better. In a matter of time, David started outperforming his peers.

This marked improvement was noticed by Peter and other people in the management. David's performance was above everyone's expectations. He received a promotion at a point when he least expected it.

David expanded his circle of influence and elicited the desired behavior in Peter by working on what was in his control, namely, his performance.

If you are in a situation where you have been trying to influence someone and haven't had much luck, you can expand your circle of influence by asking these questions:

1. What exactly do you want from the person?
2. What are the three things that lie inside your circle of influence that you can work on?
3. How will working on these three areas impact the person you are trying to influence into giving you what you want?
4. What actions can you take on these areas right away?

(Download the complete list of *powerful self-coaching questions* along with the *Being Yourself Journal* on romasharma.com)

11

7 BEST PRACTICES TO STOP WORRYING ABOUT OTHERS

Our personalities are formed cumulatively as a result of what we do on a daily basis. Any change that we want in our life can be achieved by making small changes to what we do every day. Hence, if we want to design a life in which we are more comfortable with ourselves and worry less about what others think, we need to change some things we do regularly inside our mind. We will go over 7 best practices that will help us loosen the coupling between our self-image and public image. They will also make it easier for us to implement our principles and focus on what's inside our circle of influence.

1. Individual Coaching Sessions

Undergo one-on-one coaching with a trained professional to equip yourself with the necessary skills to deal with people whom you find challenging. If you have newly started asserting yourself you could expect some pushback from them. Especially, if the equation was one in which you did most of the adjusting. You will need to take more care of yourself till people get accustomed to the changes. Seek support from a coach who can work with you through this phase.

Consult someone who is competent, compassionate and can help you explore solutions that are good for you. Avoid consulting your friends and family members for the following reasons:

(1) They might not take the time and effort to understand your situation completely.

(2) Their views could be colored by their judgments of you.

(3) They might not challenge your thinking patterns out of fear of spoiling their relationship with you.

Self-work needs time, effort and patience. It also needs a person who has the skills to work with you to move you towards your goals. I am often asked how one can choose a good coach. Firstly, *good* is subjective to what a person is looking for. Bearing that in mind, here are some broad guidelines that you can follow while selecting a coach:

(1) Decide if you prefer a face-to-face session or an online one. Accordingly, list out the available options.

(2) Check the reviews of the coaches you have short-listed. Try to get testimonials from a person who has already worked with the coach you are considering.

(3) Undergo a few sessions with the coach and see if you would like to take it forward.

Certain coaches are booked much in advance. Getting session slots with them is difficult. If you are keen on taking sessions with them you will need to get on their waitlist as soon as possible. If you are interacting with a coaching company you will need to ensure that you communicate at least once with the coach that will be working with you. Avoid closing the deal with the salesperson before you have had a chance to talk to the coach.

It's important to remember that checking reviews is good but not a foolproof way of getting a coach who works well for you. The synergy between you and your coach will largely decide the success of your sessions and that is something that can not be predicted till you try working together. I have heard of coaches with great reviews not working out well for certain clients and vice-versa too. This just indicates that eventually experiences are subjective. So, we start with what we know and then go on to what we can find out next.

Once you have settled with a coach, it is important to make the sessions regular. I request my clients to decide the frequency of their sessions although I do recommend having at least one session per fortnight. Otherwise we tend to lose continuity and context.

At the beginning of each session, you and your coach will decide a goal for that session. At the end of each session, you will make a list of actions that you will carry out before your next session. Every session begins with a review of the actions that have been set in the previous session. This is how you keep track of your progress.

If you are working long-term with a coach you need to set monthly goals, quarterly goals and annual goals. Your goals will be in line with the changes you want to make in your life like improvement of relation-ships, developing new skills or any other personal or professional objective that you have set for yourself. You will work with your coach to come up with a plan for achieving the same. You will also decide on a metric that will indicate to you that your plan is work-ing. Let's say, I have a goal of improving my skills as a trainer. I come up with a plan of the training I can undergo, the books I can read and the seniors I can request for supervision in order to improve my training skills. The measure of this plan working could be the feedback I receive from my trainees or an increase in the number of training assignments.

In some other cases, the metric might not be as tangible. For example, if I want to improve a certain relationship it might be difficult to know exactly what has to happen for me to conclude that the relationship has improved. However, if you work with your coach you can devise your own ways to measure this. For instance, I know that a relationship is going well if I feel relaxed or happy in the presence of the person.

Once your coaching sessions become regular, pause periodically every month, and see the direction in which your sessions are headed. Use your metric to check if your sessions are moving you towards your goals or not. Simple measures such as these will help you make the most of your sessions.

2. Undergo Training

If you are interested in personal growth, it helps to undergo training with mental health professionals, coaches or other experts in the field of emotional wellbeing. While selecting a training program you need to evaluate which area you would like to explore in depth. You can take up courses that teach Transactional Analysis, Neuro-Linguistic Programming, Cognitive Behavior Therapy or any other study which helps you understand yourself better. The choice of the course will depend on your area of interest.

After you have decided on a course, you will need to do some research on the trainers who are available. Today we have options of learning from online courses as well as through contact programs. You can select one that works well for you and evaluate the reviews of the trainers you are considering. I would also recommend checking the qualification of the trainers who trained your trainer. In other words, you need to look into whom the trainer learned from and which board he is certified from. Along with that, if you can contact the people who have trained with this trainer and get a first-hand testimonial that would be ideal. Careful consideration is necessary because you are not just selecting a trainer, you are choosing a certain direction and that direction has to be right for you.

Training in groups has a number of advantages. Group work helps in catching your blind spots and learning from the life stories of others as well. When the group, under the supervision of a qualified trainer, processes situations there can be incredible takeaways for everybody.

I usually conduct training programs for groups of sizes anywhere between 8-25 participants. I find the smaller groups of 10 people to be ideal as I am able to give each participant individual attention. Groups that are larger than 20 don't have that advantage although they get the benefit of meeting more people and enjoying diverse experiences.

Group learning can be a fun activity too. I have noticed that participants in these programs are happy to meet like-minded people. Many of them stay in touch long after the program is over. They also enter *budding coaching* programs after they complete their training.

Buddy Coaching is about two people who decide to share their goals and be accountable to each other as they move forward. They periodically follow up on what the other person is doing and whether or not the *buddy* is on track with respect to the predetermined plan. This also gives them an opportunity to exercise the skills they picked up during the training program.

Buddy coaching is about you being accountable to your buddy but actually it's a way of being accountable to yourself. If you do not have a coach and want a reasonable way of staying on track, this method works quite well.

3. Journal Your Thoughts

Journaling on a daily basis is a great way to understand yourself better and measure the progress in your personal development over a period of time. If you find your thoughts drifting into others' perception of you, refocus them back to yourself by journaling the situation:

"What am I worried about?"

"What do I think they want?"

"What would happen if I did what I wanted?"

Life is full of things that we imagine, most of which never come to pass. If you feel worried about something that is going to happen in the future, journal it. Write down what you think is going to happen preferably with a date by when you expect it to happen. When that date arrives, check if what you imagined actually happened or not. Write down any other observations about the situation. Over a few months of recording this information you will have sufficient evidence to indicate that many of the things you worried about actually never happened

Today's Date	What am I worried about?	Date by which I expect this to happen	Did it happen?

Whenever you feel worried about something, open this journal and read it. It will give you a reason to challenge your worry.

It is a useful practice to journal your strengths and your accomplishments as well. When you are feeling happy about something you did well, note it down in your journal. Whenever you feel demotivated, open this section and read it. You will be reminded of your special qualities and will be motivated to continue working on your goals.

If you are taking individual coaching sessions, then your journal will be very useful to refer to before a session. It will help you decide on what you should discuss with your coach and measure your progress since you last met. Hence, it is important to maintain your journal.

Download the *Being Yourself Journal* which includes powerful self-coaching questions on my site romasharma.com.

4. Observe your Self-Talk

We have two personalities inside of us—one that speaks in a gentle, loving manner to us and the other that is critical of us. The critical inner voice gives us the stick when we do something that is not in accordance with what we expect of ourselves. Based on how we were spoken to in our growing years, this voice could be gentle or harsh on us.

Be mindful of how you speak to yourself all day along. How are your words? How is your tonality? Ensure that you speak to yourself in a loving and kind way especially when you make a mistake.

Critical self-talk: *"Look, you made a mistake! Everyone noticed it. When will you learn?"*

Gentle self-talk: *"It's ok to make a mistake. It's ok if others noticed it. I learnt something from it and I will do better next time."*

We don't make mistakes by deciding to do so. Things happen. Learning from situations and letting go can greatly relieve us from the anxiety that comes with thinking that we are inept in some way.

Be mindful of how you create your body image. Avoid criticizing your size, shape, color, dimensions, face symmetry or anything else you don't like about yourself. Whenever you look at yourself in the mirror, remind yourself of your special qualities.

Instead of giving out a signal of *'please love me'*, when a person gives out a signal which says, *'I am lovable'* it is alluring.

When you like and accept yourself other people are influenced into doing so too. Feeling great about yourself lies in your circle of influence. It is something you can do, irrespective of what others think of you.

Silence your inner critic which says you can't, the voice that runs like background noise forcing you to care more about others. Your new inner voice can be trained, through awareness and practice, to support you unconditionally. It prevents comparison and a feeling of inadequacy. It allows you to make mistakes and learn from them. It rejoices in your special qualities and lets you be who you are irrespective of what others want you to believe.

Through your self-talk, give yourself permission and freedom to be yourself:

"It's ok for me to be me."

"It's ok to have needs."

"It's ok to make mistakes."

"It's ok if other people become angry with me."

One of the best ways to change the way you speak to yourself is to journal your self-talk and process it in your coaching sessions.

Once you wholeheartedly love yourself you will be able to deal with anything that comes with being *you*. Don't you easily support the ones you love?

5. Design an Environment of Self-care

When I tell my clients that taking care of themselves first is important before taking care of other people I sometimes receive this response, *"I can't care for myself first. That's selfish."*

When I ask them what they want, they tell me what others want. When I ask them what their goals are, they tell me what others want them to do. They might be discounting the fact that they *do* have a life of their own.

There are many different ways in which we could convince ourselves that taking care of ourselves before others is a selfish thing to do. Even people who understand this concept at some level tend to berate themselves when they aren't able to meet the expectations that others have of them.

There is usually a strong parental message that gets absorbed in childhood that could lead to this belief:

"Caring for yourself is selfish."

"You can only be happy when others are happy."

"You are ok if others are ok with you."

People who try too hard to make others happy are usually the unhappiest from within. They tend to lash out at their loved ones, thereby creating a spiral downward of greater misery for themselves and ironically the ones they care for the most.

We can not happily do things for others while we are unhappy deep down inside.

Self-care is not optional. We owe it to ourselves and to the people around us.

You can work out ways to ask people for what you need without feeling guilty for having needs. For example, you can take a day off if you feel consumed by your work pressure and need to relax or you can consider joining a class that helps you explore an area of your interest.

Surround yourself with people with whom you feel happy. If you repeatedly feel drained by being around certain people who make you feel less than positive about yourself, then it's time to create some distance —physically or mentally. When people treat you poorly it indicates more about them than it does about you. You can avoid using their views to appraise yourself.

We become an average of the five people we spend the most time with. So we need to choose our company carefully. Find people who don't worry about others' perceptions and strive out of their comfort zones to become better versions of themselves. Surround yourself with people who are hardworking, action-oriented, goal-oriented or any other quality that you like. Even if you already have these qualities, you will benefit from the influence of your companions.

An environment of self-care is not something that will develop on its own. It has to be created by deciding to do so and proactively taking action. It usually gets neglected amidst busy schedules unless it is prioritized. A good thought to affirm to yourself is, *"It is important for me to take care of myself."*

6. Meditation

A majority of my clients have observed significant improvement in their emotional wellbeing by meditating for just 20 minutes in a day. Like an engine needs some downtime to work to its optimum level, our mind needs a break to focus better too. Meditation is a way to take a break from whatever is happening around us. It helps to rejuvenate ourselves.

Care needs to be taken to not force ourselves to do this consciously. If you do not feel like meditating and if you forcibility try to meditate, it will cause your body to resist the process. So being relaxed and interested in engaging with the process is a great starting point.

Sit down in a place where you will not be disturbed. Close your eyes. Breathe slowly and deeply while focusing on your breath. Allow thoughts to pass through your mind without judging them or trying to control them.

Set a time aside in a day and a place where you will meditate. Stick to the same time and place so that it becomes a part of your unconscious process. If you are new to meditation, you can start with 10 minutes a day and slowly increase it to 20 minutes or more.

You also have the option of using guided meditation tapes or music. There are many different types of meditation. You can explore till you find one that works well for you.

It is essential to make meditation a daily practice. More so, if the goal is to reduce overthinking.

You will begin to see reduced anxiety and improved concentration within two weeks of daily meditation. Over time, this practice will become easy and you will notice being more relaxed and calm inside your mind even if the external situations are not as you want them to be.

7. Visualize Your Outcomes

In my training programs, often participants ask me what they should do to have more confidence. I tell them that confidence is not something you *have*, it's something you *do*. It's a mental process. If I start describing confidence to you in a way that you can recognize it, you will start feeling confident too. Hence, it is more to do with what you imagine inside your mind and how you talk to yourself that decides whether you will feel confident or not. If I am about to give a speech and before going on stage, I remember all the times when I blanked out in front of an audience and forgot my lines, will I be able to speak confidently? Probably not.

The mental movies that you play are largely responsible for how you feel. You can tap into your state of confidence by remembering the episodes when you were confidently able to do something. If there is a situation that is coming up in the future which you believe is challenging for you—maybe you have to confront someone or make a request to a person who you think is difficult to handle—you can enter a state of mind where you create an image of yourself speaking confidently to this person. When you imagine something, you are creating neural pathways inside your mind that strengthen that particular behavior. When the situation presents itself, you will feel like you are doing it for the second time and so it will be a lot easier.

When I speak of visualization techniques a frequently asked question is, *"I can not get things by just visualizing them inside my mind."*

Visualization is not to be confused with being inactive. You would not be reading this book if I merely visualized you reading it. I had to take the required actions so that the book gets created and reaches you. Actions are required to manifest our thoughts into things. At the same time our visualization of being successful is the first step. It ensures that we have sufficient motivation to execute our plans to the best of our abilities. It also gives us a blueprint of precisely what we want which makes it easier for us to go after it.

Pause for a moment and imagine yourself being relaxed despite the judgments of others. Visualize yourself confidently advancing towards your goals and living the life of your dreams. How exactly is your life in this visualization? Perceiving it is the first step towards achieving it.

12

AFTERWORD

Our public image is important to us. Our reptilian brain ensures we care for what others think of us. At the same time how much we care for others versus ourselves needs to be in balance for us to experience peace.

Having an emotional need to please people at our expense rarely gets us their love and respect. It could make them take us for granted. When we go out of our way to do things for people we expect more from them as well. They may or may not live up to these expectations, leading to disappointment.

If we end up doing something we don't want to do, solely with the intention of pleasing others, we need to take responsibility for that action. Taking responsibility prevents us from blaming others or feeling sorry for ourselves.

We fear being judged and rejected by people. We fear moving out of our comfort zone as we don't want to disturb others or invoke their insecurities. These fears stop us from moving forward with conviction. They can be dealt with by processing with a trained professional, writing a journal, practicing meditation and by using visualization techniques.

Dealing with our fears is necessary to become unstoppable when it comes to following our dreams. At the end of our lives, we don't regret the things we didn't accomplish. We regret the things we didn't even try. When we look back we want to remember an amazing life we designed for ourselves and lived to the fullest.

We have a certain amount of energy that we need to carry out our daily tasks effectively. We can not possibly care for everything that happens as it will drain our mental faculties. Imagine a car with a limited amount of fuel. You need to drive it with care. If you drive it around even when it's not required, you will run out of fuel and will not have any when you really need it.

Your care and attention is similar to that fuel. If you care for everything that happens to you or every person who comes along your way, you will soon be depleted of your limited energy and will not have any of it left when something important requires your attention. Hence, your ability to decide what to care for, when and by how much will largely determine the quality of your life. Your principles will make it easier for you to make this decision. Establish a strong set of principles that serve you well, stay focused on what is inside your circle of influence and watch your dream life manifest.

In this book, we have gone over many ways to take charge of our lives and be ourselves authentically and unapologetically. The benefits you will get from these methods largely depend on how much action you take on them.

Action leads to confidence and certainty.

You are confident that you can brush your teeth because you did it many times before. It is an action you can easily replicate if you wanted to. The mental states that support that action have developed and you can tap into them at any time. In the same way, you can gain the confidence to do anything you want by repeatedly doing it.

The more actions you take, the more confident you become and vice versa too. This feedback loop strengthens over time. To see results you will need to take action on the practices that have been suggested in this book.

Observe which practices get you good results and do more of those. The mental states that support your desired version of yourself will strengthen over time and before you know it you would have already made that change.

To Your Success,

Roma

Please Review This Book

We have reached the end of the book and I sincerely hope that you found value in it. I have a request for you. If you liked the book would you please let others know about it?

1. Please leave a review on an online store that is convenient for you. (If you log onto romasharma.com and click on the book, you will find the list of storefronts where it is available.)
2. Share it on Facebook, Twitter, Instagram, Pinterest, or LinkedIn
3. Please mention it to your circle of family, friends, or colleagues

Reviews help readers discover books they like. They are the best way to get the word out. Even a line or two of your views on the book will help.

Thank you for taking the time to do this. Your support is much appreciated. I look forward to reading your views.

ABOUT THE AUTHOR

Roma Sharma is a Certified Coach and Trainer who has been working in the field of emotional well-being since 2014. She runs a training company that authors programs for people from a variety of backgrounds—IT Industry, Educational Institutions, Counseling Academies, and Hospitality Industry to name a few. She works with organizations to design programs that specifically address their training needs.

Roma has a keen interest in understanding human behavior and connecting with people at a deeper level. Besides training and coaching, she regularly hosts a meetup in her city to discuss various topics related to mental health.

She likes to take up issues that her audience members experience in their day-to-day life and provide them with clarity so that they devise simple solutions that work well for them. She has had the privilege of watching her clients become very successful in attaining the transformation that they set out to achieve.

When she is not training, she loves to bake cakes, read books, and play with cats.

Credentials:

- B.E (CSE)
- Diploma in Counselling Skills, person-centered therapy
- International Certification in Transactional Analysis 101
- Foundation course in Transactional Analysis
- Master practitioner of NLP (ABNLP), NLP Trainer
- Advanced Diploma in Hypnosis (Business-NLP, UK)

Do you also want to overcome negativity and find happiness in yourself? The book, **What Will Make You Happy?** gives you simple ways to cut the downward spirals of stress and create lasting happiness.

What readers say about the book:

"A must-read for a meaningful and happy life"

"A fabulous read with relatable examples and anecdotes"

Log onto romasharma.com and buy your copy of **What Will Make You Happy?** today!

ONLINE COURSES

The Complete Guide to Finding Your Perfect Partner

Would you like to have lifetime access to my video training courses at 80% OFF? Please find the discount coupons here:

romasharma.com/courses

STAY IN TOUCH

Here are the best ways to stay in touch with me:

Subscribe to my Newsletter

Please leave your mail ID at **romasharma.com/newsletter** to receive articles on the best coaching practices, free video training programs and eBooks.

Like my Facebook Page

Hit the *like* button on my Author Page **facebook.com/romasharmawriter** to receive the latest news from the world of coaching and the best offers on my new releases.

DOWNLOAD YOUR FREE 'BEING YOURSELF JOURNAL'

I hope you have downloaded your copy of the journal. If you have not, here it is again.

Your FREE Book!

For more books log onto
romasharma.com

The **Being Yourself Journal** with powerful self-coaching questions is available at **romasharma.com**

Here is what you will find in the journal:

1. Page templates you can fill out every day to connect with your thoughts and feelings
2. Affirmations to increase self-esteem and confidence
3. Self-coaching questions that will help you find solutions in difficult situations
4. Simple ways to decrease worry and stay calm in the present moment

Journaling is a powerful way to understand yourself better. The way you feel about your thoughts changes when you write them down. If you journal on a regular basis you will find that—in a matter of time—your journal will become the single most useful document you have on yourself.

Whether you need to find a solution to a problem or just vent out your feelings, your journal is available to you whenever you need it. Download your copy and start journaling today.

Download now! Log onto **romasharma.com**

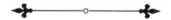

Made in United States
Orlando, FL
10 April 2024

45640201R00075